My Dad's
Rose

To –

God bless!

[signature]

Jeffrey F. Joutras

My Dad's
Rose

*One son's struggle with
his father's tragic death*

gatekeeper press
Columbus, Ohio

My Dad's Rose: One son's struggle with his father's tragic death

Published by Gatekeeper Press
2167 Stringtown Rd, Suite 109
Columbus, OH 43123-2989
www.GatekeeperPress.com

ISBN (paperback): 9781642374858
eISBN: 9781642374865

Dedication

For my dad, I miss you and I love you; I really do.

To all who struggle with the loss of a
loved one, especially for men who are
grieving the loss of their father.

Acknowledgements

For those who will read this book and gain some measure of value from it, no matter how small. And to those who purchase it as a gift or recommend it to others, so it may help them deal with the loss of their loved one, thank you.

To my youngest son John, who helped immensely with the editing of this book and for his insights in helping me develop my story. Thank you, Johnny!

For my family, I love you all very much and hope that you know the love in my heart for each of you.

Author's Note

As a family, we would visit this artesian well near our home in Pilcher Park called the Flowing Well. We'd fill up bottles with fresh well water and often go there just to get a refreshing drink on a hot summer day. A portion of the net proceeds from the sale of this book will be donated, in memory of my father, to help fund building a water project in a portion of the world that desperately needs clean water. This is one small way I hope to honor my father's memory and to help others in need. The organization is **charity:water** (www.charitywater. org) which does a lot of work in developing countries. Please consider making an additional direct donation to charitywater.org.

Table of Contents

Introduction

The greatest good is what
we do for one another.

— Mother Theresa

his is the story of my dad's tragic death which occurred in 1975 when I was 14 years old and my memory around the events of that day. I share my struggles of living without him while growing up and describe the challenges I've experienced as an adult in coming to terms with his passing. My father, Louis Joutras, was involved in an industrial accident that took his life at the age of 48, leaving my mom, six sons and one daughter behind.

If you are reading this book, you may have lost a loved one yourself, perhaps a parent or close family member or friend. I hope that you gain some valuable insight from my struggles and hope that what I share can help you in your situation, whatever that may be.

A large portion of this book is based around the eulogy that our high school principal and Catholic priest, Father Roger Kaffer, gave at my dad's funeral Mass. I was inspired to write this book, in part, because of his sermon. While the passages are very personal to me and my family, I share them because they are beautifully written, and I feel they should be shared outside our family circle. I also share some of the challenges I've had as an adult while finally coming to grips with his death while I suffered through depression for a period of years. Even though it took nearly four decades, I've learned how to honor his memory during this process and have come to understand more about myself, my dad's life and his passing.

If my personal story helps just one person, then my purpose and mission in writing this book will have been met. God bless you for reading it.

Fisk's Home Run

I knew it was gonna go out. It was just a question of it being fair or foul.

—Carlton Fisk

Game Six of the 1975 World Series between the Boston Red Sox and the Cincinnati Reds is one of the most famous games in World Series history. It's famous because of catcher Carlton Fisk's iconic, game-ending 12th inning home run. Fisk hit a high fly ball down the left foul line and, not knowing whether it would stay fair, he jumped up, motioning with both arms for it to stay fair. And it did! Fisk ran the bases clapping and jumping up and down. I will always remember that game because it was played the night before my dad was killed in a workplace accident. The game was played on October 21, 1975. Not that I watched the game or anything, because the game ended well after midnight and I was in bed. I was a freshman in high school at the time; it was a Tuesday night, a school night. Boston won the game 7-6 on Fisk's home run to force a seventh game with Cincinnati. If you aren't familiar with this historic home run you can watch it on YouTube or do a search on the internet to see some of the famous pictures of Fisk urging his home run to stay fair. It has its place in baseball history.

When I was in my forties, I remember watching TV in my bedroom one day, when my daughter Aimee (who was 15 or 16 at the time) came in and a film clip came up showing Fisk's famous home run. I told Aimee that I knew the exact date that home run took place. She asked how I knew that, and I told her: "the very next day your grandfather was killed in an explosion and fire at work." And that I would always remember that famous home run and what day it happened for that very reason.

After I told her that little story, she got up from the room and left. I could tell something wasn't right with her. I found her in her bedroom with tears in her eyes. When I asked her what was wrong, she said that she was sad because of what had happened to my dad. I told her I wished that she could have met him and gotten to know him. It's one of the things that always hurts the most, the fact that none of my children or my wife ever got to meet my father. I think he would have been an awesome grandfather and father-in-law.

Sports were a big part of my family life growing up. My brothers and I each participated in one or more sports, including baseball, football, wrestling or even basketball. We played these sports around the house, from grade school and all throughout high school. Going to my brother's games, if I didn't have one of my own to go to, was common while growing up. Baseball was the biggest sport for all of us, with Little League, Pony League, Colt League, and high-school and college baseball all being a part of what one or more of us six boys participated in.

When it came to professional baseball, my parents were Chicago White Sox fans. All five of my brothers were White Sox fans and my sister was too. I was the only Chicago Cubs fan in the family! As the only Cubs fan, I got teased a lot—and I mean a lot—as a young-ster. When I was eight years old, the Cubs collapsed after leading their division by eight games in August 1969 and lost their chance at the pennant. The next few years they didn't fare much better, which led to more teas-ing. The Cubs just kept on losing. Ron Santo, who was the Cubs' all-star third baseman, was my favorite player growing up, and I got teased for that too! I remember my dad coming home from work one day and giving me a baseball signed by many of the Cubs' starting play-ers, including Fergie Jenkins, Glenn Beckert and Ron Santo. My dad got it from a friend who went to the game. It's a keepsake I have to this day. Knowing my dad got that baseball for me is pretty special.

There are many events and specific dates that stick with us during our lifetimes, some rewarding, some sad, and Fisk's famous home run is one of those for me. I vaguely remember hearing that my dad was happy about Fisk's home run. I believe he came home late from a meeting or work and may have even seen it on television. I don't know, since it occurred after midnight. The next day, my world, and our family's world, changed forever.

Sister Remi's Class

I close my eyes and I see your face, if home's where my heart is . . . then I'm out of place, Lord won't you give me strength to make it through somehow, I've never been more homesick than now.

—Mercy Me

I was sitting in Sister Remi's religion class, room 107, when the call came over the intercom. It was the associate principal, Sister Julia, speaking. "Sister Remi, is Jeff Joutras in your class? Can you send him down to my office?" I was a freshman at Providence High School in New Lenox, Illinois and was sixth in the line of Joutrases who had attended the high school. My five older siblings preceded me, and my younger brother would attend Providence the next year. Sister Remi was also my homeroom teacher, in addition to being my religion teacher. She was one of the many nuns from the Dominican order from Nashville, Tennessee who taught at Providence High School.

Sr. Remi said, "Yes, he's here. I'll send him down."

Many of my classmates oohed and ahhed, saying things like, *"What did you do Jeff? You're in trouble now!"* and teasing me. I didn't really know what to think. Why would I be getting called down to the office in the middle of class? So, I grabbed my books and walked down the hallway to the associate principal's office located in the center of the school. Sister Remi's classroom was at the far west side of the school; I had a little time to think on the walk. It was a strange feeling to walk the empty hallways during the middle of a class period. I felt like I wasn't really supposed to be there; it was eerily quiet walking past the other classroom doorways. I had no idea why I had been summoned to the associate principal's office. I just did as I was told.

I stepped into Sr. Julia's office. My older brother Ron, who was a senior, was sitting there. I looked at him, not sure what was going on and wondered why he was there, too. I sat down next to him with my books in hand. The Dean of Students was in the office with Sister Julia. I don't recall the words she used or how she even prefaced what she had to say, but she was the one who told us Dad was dead. Killed, in a work accident at Union Oil in Romeoville, Illinois. The date was October 22, 1975.

All I can recall next is walking out the front of the school on the sidewalk, books still in my hands, crying. The Dean and my brother Ron were there next to me. The Dean tried to console me, saying something to the effect of: "Now don't cry; your dad would want you to take it like a man." Even then, I thought that was an insensitive comment. Perhaps he didn't know what else to say. I was only 14 years old. I didn't know what was going on. I had just been told we lost our father, and he's telling me to *take it like a man*?

My cousin Tim Ruettiger drove Ron and me home. Tim coached football and wrestling and also taught physical education and history at the high school. I remember looking out the car window on the drive home and thinking what a beautiful fall day it was. The trees were in fall colors with red, yellow and orange leaves. It was an unusually warm and sunny day for the last part of October. When we got home, I took off my shoes like I always did and went upstairs to my bedroom. Sitting on the bunkbed, I just stared out the window and waited. I didn't know what to do, other than sit and wait for everybody else to come home. I don't remember a whole lot more. I do remember thinking it was a really nice day, weather-wise. I know that may seem strange to you; it's just one of those things that's stuck with me.

First Pew

My Father didn't tell me how to live.
He lived; and let me watch him do it.

—Clarence Kelland

"The only reason for our life on earth is to get to heaven. Last Saturday morning at our varsity football Mass, that's what I told the team and coaches before the Providence-Aurora game. Last Saturday, that game seemed awfully important (and it was, but only in a relative way). Lou, and many of you here today, watched that game. There's another game today – against Walter Lutheran, and many of you had planned to watch that game today, but you aren't. You're here instead, and rightly so. Because football games, and everything else we do on earth, are only relatively important."

Our family was seated in the first-row pew, directly in front of the lectern on the left side of

St. Bernard's Church when looking at the altar. St. Bernard's in Joliet, Illinois was our family parish. We were there for the funeral Mass of my father on Saturday, October 25, 1975. My brother Mike was sitting beside me with the rest of our family. I really don't remember a whole lot about the Mass except for the homily that Father Kaffer gave and I do remember my brother next to me crying, with his hands covering his face at times. I can hear and remember, to this very day, Fr. Kaffer's words, his intonation and cadence. It's a strange thing . . . many other details from that important day in our family's life have completely escaped me.

Father Kaffer was the principal at Providence Catholic High School at that time. My brother Ron was a senior and I was a freshman. We both played high school football and our football games back in the 1970s were played on Saturdays. Father Kaffer and my dad were the same age, and both graduated from Joliet Township High School (now Joliet Central) in the same year. They were friends and they had a connection that went way back. I remember Dad telling him he'd be the next bishop in the diocese of Joliet and even teasing Fr. Kaffer about that. Fr. Kaffer did eventually become Auxiliary Bishop of Joliet later in his life, albeit not the "next bishop." Fr. Kaffer used to visit all the Providence families once a year, which in and of itself spoke a lot to his dedication to the school and the families. I remember him visiting and playing ping pong with us in our basement. Dad had renovated it into a recreation room a year or two before and we spent time watching TV and playing games there. Fr. Kaffer was a very down-to-earth guy. I thought it was a pretty cool thing that a principal and priest would play ping pong with us.

The opening to his homily has resonated with me for many reasons as I've gotten older. I distinctly remember his words about what we do on earth being *"only relatively important."* As a teenager, I didn't completely grasp the meaning of his message at the time. As I've matured and grown older, I've reflected on my values from years ago and the things I used to value have changed. Now that I'm in my fifties, the things I thought were important five, ten or even twenty years ago are no longer as important to me. I think that's one thing Fr. Kaffer was trying to teach us, that there is certainly way more to life and way more important things than football games. Cheering on my favorite sports teams or making the all-important sale or getting the next promotion were things that had seemed really important to me before, but they're not nearly as important now, especially as I've reflected on life on earth and life in the hereafter. The importance of things that once seemed really critical in the moment has diminished as time has faded. Thinking back on how emotionally vested I've been in sporting events or decisions at work in the past only serve to prove Fr. Kaffer's point that those things are only relatively important.

> *"The only really important thing we have to do in our whole life, the only reason for our life on earth, is to get to heaven. If you*

do that, your life is a success. If you don't, regardless of what else you may accomplish, you're a failure. It is only in this context of faith that this week's events can have any meaning at all. As Cardinal Suhard said, 'A Christian is one whose life would not make sense if God did not exist.' Lou Joutras' life and death would not make sense if God did not exist.

"This doesn't answer all our questions today, and don't wait with bated breath for me to answer them this morning, because I don't have all the answers, but I do have a few reflections I'd like to share with you. The first is this: if you or I were God, we would not be here this morning because you or I would not have permitted Lou Joutras to be where he was, when he was, on Wednesday.

"But then I think we must also admit that if you or I were God we would never have permitted the crucifixion, and once again we would not be here this morning. But thank God, God is God—and we are not, because there never could have been an Easter Sunday, with its chance for heaven for Lou and you and me, if there had not been a Good Friday."

There are lots of things about life and death and God and religion that are difficult for me to comprehend. I do know that for sure I'd be in a whole worse mess if I didn't believe in God and have faith in Him and hope for heaven. Sitting there in that front pew, Fr. Kaffer's words impacted me in a significant way. A chance for heaven for you and me, that's all I think any of us can hope for and pray for. It's what I pray for.

After the funeral Mass, we went out to Resurrection Cemetery in Romeoville, Illinois for the final chapel ceremony. I remember the long line of cars that seemed to go on forever while we made our way out there from the church. We came from a big family, had a lot of relatives and Dad clearly knew a lot of people. The church was packed on that Saturday for his funeral Mass. There was a great show of support for us with the tremendous turnout that day. It was a sunny day, in contrast to the previous day at my dad's wake when it rained continuously. I remember sitting in the front row of the chapel and since Dad served in the Army, his casket was draped with a U.S. flag and a soldier played "Taps" on the bugle at the end of the ceremony. I remember the flag that covered my dad's casket being taken off and folded up and given to my mom. There is a very specific way the soldiers fold the flag so that it ends up in a neatly folded triangle. That was a really sad thing to see as a teenager, kind of like it was all finally sinking in, when the two soldiers gave the flag to my mom. It was heartbreaking and I really felt bad for her. Whenever I hear "Taps" being played, it brings back memories of that day at the chapel.

Later that night or the next night, I can remember sitting on the living room floor opening up all of the cards we got from our friends and relatives from the wake and reading them. There were lots of cards to open! I remember thinking that my dad could be walking in the front door at any time. But of course, he didn't. It was a strange feeling, suddenly someone who's with you all the time is not there anymore, with no hope they ever will again.

There was a lot of support from friends and relatives when Dad passed away. We had a lot of visitors for a while. But soon, everyone had to go on living their normal lives. The visitors became less and less, and I think that's when it got really hard for us, especially for Mom. That's when things became even more real and surreal, somehow all at the same time. We were dealing with the day to day and carrying on with our lives as best we could.

My Mother, My Hero

*Watching someone you love suffer
is worse than suffering yourself.*

—Author Unknown

As I reflect on the first few years after Dad passed away, I vividly remember the pain, suffering, and loneliness Mom felt. I know many times she was grieving while trying to keep it all together. Even though I lived in the same house and was with her often, I couldn't imagine what she was going through. At this time, Mom worked at the Will County Courthouse and she continued working while I was in high school and after I went away to college. She kept herself somewhat busy by joining the local bicycle club and going on bike rides with that group. Even though many times I'm sure she didn't feel like it, she went. She wrote a nice article for the bike club newsletter at the end of the first year she joined, thanking the members for being so supportive and nice to her, and especially for staying with her if she lagged behind on the rides. I joined the bike club also and went on some rides with her during this time. She also volunteered at the local Veterans of Foreign Wars post, working their fish fry dinners on Friday evenings, serving as a waitress and bussing tables.

Each day, my mom would wake up my brother Mark and I to get ready for school. We'd come down from our upstairs bedroom and eat breakfast at the kitchen counter. After getting us off to school, Mom would go to work at the courthouse and then she would be back midafternoon when we arrived home after classes were out. She went about doing all the things she used to do, although now she was raising us alone.

One specific memory I have is going on a guided bus trip to New Orleans with Mom and my younger brother Mark in August 1977, right before the new school year. Prior to Dad's death, we would always take a family camping vacation each year. With Dad gone, she decided on this bus trip, something we'd never done before. I don't recall a lot of details about the trip, but I remember that Elvis Presley died while we were in Louisiana, so we purchased a newspaper and read the details of what happened. My mom and dad were the same age, 48, when my dad died, so my mom had a lot of years ahead of her. Today, my beautiful mother is 91 years old, and although she has had a couple of strokes and is suffering from the symptoms of dementia, she seems to be happy most days, and for that I am grateful.

I remember another time, maybe a year or two after my dad's passing, specifically talking to her when she was down and worried about what others were going to think because she needed to buy a new car. She was afraid to buy one, fearful of what others would say, as if it wasn't right that she was spending my dad's life insurance money on a new vehicle. I remember her brother, my Uncle Dewey, telling her to get the car and not to worry about what others thought or said. It's a difficult thing, bearing the burden of worrying about what others will think or say about you. I know my mom struggled with that and I have, too. What will others think about me if I publicize that I suffered from depression for some time? Those negative thoughts can be paralyzing.

I remember Mom seeing an ad in a religious magazine about a group needing rosaries, so she replied to the ad. She soon received rosary kits in the mail and started making them to send them to this group. It's one of the things my mom did to keep herself busy. The kit had beads, metal wire and crosses in it. The Rosary is prayed by saying a group of prayers including the Our Father, Hail Mary, and the Glory Be, all while moving along the beads to keep track of where you are in the process. There are five groupings, called decades, which include ten beads each. If you aren't familiar with what a rosary looks like, it is comprised of a crucifix, groups of beads held together by metal wire or string and a nice medal, usually with an image of Jesus Christ or Mary on the medal. That medal connects all the five decades together. When I look back at this simple volunteer act my mom did, it impresses me. Not only was she trying to stay busy doing something, but she did something of value that would help others . . . and helping others pray is an awesome thing. I recall her sitting at the dinner table after supper putting the rosaries together or often sitting on the end of the sofa in the family room while working on them. She used a small pliers to bend the metal wire while balancing a box of beads on her lap. One of my most prized possessions to this day is a rosary she made especially for me. Another thing that my mom did was collect religious magazines and she'd send them over to the missionaries in India. Mailing religious magazines overseas was something she did on a regular basis, I believe it was part of her own effort to make a small difference in the world. She tried to do little things when she wasn't at work to keep herself busy and productive to take her mind off the grief.

My mom was the original example of journaling in my life. She wrote a lot and has quite a few notebooks of her writings from the mid-1970s and on. Today, you read about creating the habit of writing in a journal . . . or journaling. It's a whole industry unto itself. It used to be called writing in a diary. Perhaps the term "journaling" is supposed to sound more appealing to the masses or more sophisticated. I am sure she wrote a lot about what was happening in her life and also about what she was thinking and feeling, as I believe it was her way of dealing with her grief. I haven't read my mom's journals out of respect for her privacy and she hasn't shared them with our family. I know at some point when she's gone from this earth, I'll have an opportunity to read what she wrote and that will give me a whole different perspective into what Mom was thinking and feeling during those years. I believe writing was therapeutic for her. I know my mom often suffered in silence, and I believe she wrote in her notebooks as a way to cope with her grief. It pained me to see her suffer then and it hurts even now. Now, she'll ask about what happened to my dad—"that guy," she says. I have to tell her what happened, and she'll say, "That's right." Because of her memory loss, in a way, it's a bit like living the whole event over and over again.

I do believe one of the ways to better deal with grief or sadness or depression is to talk about it, to write down your thoughts, to talk to others, to share your experiences. We don't have to bear life's burdens on our own; there are people who can help us, who can help you and me. One thing I've started doing is to write down the thoughts that come into my head that don't serve me and to also write down the thoughts that do serve me. By writing my thoughts down, I can deal with them and combat negative thinking by seeing how illogical they are and better embrace the good thoughts. Writing helped my mom deal with her grief—it's helped me too. I learned this from the example my mother gave me, although it took me decades to take up the exercise. As her journaling was an important aspect in her dealing with her loss so perhaps it will help me continue to deal with my thoughts and feelings as well.

A Poem for Mom

*Write hard and clear
about what hurts.*

—Ernest Hemingway

I wrote a poem for Mom late in the summer of 1979, right before leaving for my freshman year of college. My plans were to attend Augustana College in Rock Island, Illinois for three years and then Duke University for two years. During my senior year in high school and the summer after graduation, one of my friends and I were writing poems about different experiences we were having. Most of the poems we wrote were just silly reflections on what was happening to us. I got the idea to write a poem about my dad and leave it as a gift along with a card for my mom. I received a reply in the mail from her shortly after being at college thanking me for the card and poem. My mom still has the poem proudly displayed in her bedroom:

My Dad

Do the passing days heal the wounds of sorrow?
Who can we turn to? To whom can we go?
We look to God today,
He'll show us the way to go.

He went very unexpectedly; not leaving any warning,
He left all of us behind,
We think of him always,
Because he's ever present on our minds.

Gone at the age of 48,
He taught us how to live,
He showed us by his example,
How we ought to give.

He gave us love and much more,
He made us laugh and made us cry,
And now he's not with us,
And we keep asking "Why?"

We know how he lived,
God gave him the strength to,
To live a life,
In the way it ought to.

He left us on a Wednesday,
It was a beautiful fall day,
That October will always be,
Because Dad went on his way.

At his wake, they waited in the rain,
To pay respects at his passing,
He's someone who will be remembered,
Because his good works are everlasting.

Never to see another family reunion,
Never to see all his kids grown,
Dad lived life to his fullest,
We must understand he was just "on loan."

Dad never thought of himself,
He always did good for others,
He could always find the time,
To solve the problems of one another.

Dad taught us right and wrong,
But we didn't always listen,
And now he's gone forever,
It's his voice that we'll be missin'.

Time keeps moving on, Dad,
But it will never fade,
Our love for you during these times
Which God has made.

Jeffrey F. Joutras

Dad, before I close this poem,
I just want to say,
We MISS you,
And we LOVE you in every way!

Your loving son,
—Jeff

Newspaper Articles

My home is in heaven; I'm just traveling through this place.

—Billy Graham

There were two articles published in Joliet's local newspaper, *The Herald-News*, regarding my dad's death. One was published the day after Dad died and the other four days later. I cut out the first article from the newspaper and have kept it as a remembrance for over 42 years. I was only recently made aware of the second article by my brother Mark, after I started seeking out more details of my father's upbringing. I am researching as much as I can about my father's life and plan to put that information together in a memorial book as a legacy to him for my siblings. I also have the newspaper clipping of my father's obituary notice. I present these two articles exactly as they were written in the paper.

We had a long family history with our local newspaper. The paper route that our older brothers had since 1965 was eventually passed down to Mark and me. My brother and I delivered over 100 newspapers every afternoon when we got home from school for the Joliet *Herald-News*. We stopped delivering newspapers after my dad died.

Jolietan killed in   Published October 24, 1975
Union Oil fire

Romeoville—A Joliet man was killed Wednesday morning in an explosion and fire at the Union Oil 76 plant at 135th Street and New Avenue.

Louis A. Joutras, 48, of Maple Road was pronounced dead at the scene by Will County Deputy Coroner William Goodale.

Two Lockport men in an oil separating pit with him at the time of the explosion were uninjured, according to Forrest Wylie, superintendent of administrative services at the plant.

Wylie said the three men were in the pit when there was "a minor explosion followed by a flash fire." Joutras, an instrument repairman, was trapped in the pit, according to Wylie.

He said the cause of the accident hasn't been determined, but that it will be investigated by plant security persons.

He also said there will be a federal investigation of the matter under the Occupational Health and Safety Act.

Wylie said Joutras' brother-in-law, Bernie Ruettiger, who is a safety inspector at the plant, was at the scene during the explosion. Joutras was a 24-year employee of Union 76.

He is survived by his widow, Elizabeth, and seven children, Mrs. Peter (Christine) Ragusa, 24, Steven, 22, Joe, 20, Mike, 19, Ronnie, 17, Jeff, 14 and Mark, 12. Mrs. Joutras is an employee of the Will County Clerk's office. He was a brother-in-law of Circuit Clerk Sam Paul.

The body was taken to the Fred C. Dames Funeral Home. Funeral services will be Saturday morning. Visitation will be from 2-4 and 7-9 Friday.

Romeoville police attempted to gain information about the explosion shortly after it happened. However, they were refused information by plant officials, according to Police Chief Fred Hayes.

County Coroner Willard Blood said officials usually don't invite police to such accident investigations since the plant has its own security department. They fear that police might obtain information from improper sources, he said. There is no chance of any type of coverup since the coroner's office is involved in such investigations, he said.

Jeffrey F. Joutras

**Union Oil 76 officials   Published October 26, 1975
explain fatal explosion**

Officials at the Union Oil 76 plant in Romeoville have clarified some aspects of an explosion and fire at the plant Wednesday morning which killed a Joliet man.

Louis A. Joutras, 48, of Maple Road, was killed while working in an oil separating pit at the refinery. He was trapped in the pit by a minor explosion and flash fire.

Plant officials originally said there were two other men in the pit but said late this week that the victim was alone in the pit.

Three other men, including Joutras' brother-in-law, Bernie Ruettiger, were standing outside the pit at the time of the explosion.

A previous report indicated Ruettiger is a safety inspector at the plant. Officials said Ruettiger was recently listed as a safety inspector, but had not yet assumed the duties.

The cause of the explosion and fire are being investigated by plant security officials and there will be a federal investigation under the Occupational Health and Safety Act.

Funeral services for Joutras were Saturday.

That was the extent of the news coverage about my father's death. There were no other follow up articles ever published.

After reading these articles again, I wish I would have talked to my Uncle Bernie about the accident, because, as the article says, he was there when it happened. Unfortunately, my uncle has long since passed away. I wonder what my uncle actually witnessed, how he might have reacted and felt knowing his brother-in-law was in that pit when the explosion and fire occurred. I imagine that it must have been a terrible burden for him to have been there on site. It must have weighed on him throughout his life.

The second article attempts to explain further details of the explosion. But it really explains nothing, it just clarifies who was in the pit and who wasn't. It makes me angry to read it. It seems like it's Union Oil covering their backsides and says nothing about the reasons behind the explosion and fire. The real reasons for the explosion probably will never be known.

I never asked my mother about the accident or what she knew either. I guess I didn't want her to have to relive the tragedy of that day; it would have been too painful. It was hard enough for her after that, and for years afterwards to get her life put back together. I had heard that my dad had first, second and third degree burns all over his body. I'm sure this is the reason he couldn't be shown at the wake and why there was a closed casket.

I've done some searching online to find out if there were any other articles or OSHA reports on the accident but haven't been able to find much additional information. OSHA was in its early stages as a federal agency, founded as an institution in 1971 by then-president Richard Nixon. So, I am sure at that time it wasn't the sophisticated and in-depth organization it is today. I imagine that if an accident of this nature happened today it would get much more press, even television and internet coverage. Recently, I discovered on the OSHA website there were two fines levied against Union Oil because of the accident. One for $600 and one for $100. There are no details as to the specifics of the fines. A whole $700 in fines in exchange for my dad's life. Freedom of Information requests to OSHA failed to yield any additional information because all the records from that timeframe were destroyed. Apparently, because of the age of the accident, OSHA didn't feel it necessary to keep the records or have them digitized and stored in some sort of retrieval system.

I thought it important to include the two newspaper articles to show what the press coverage was like back in 1975. Contrast that to any similar accident happening in today's world and you'd have a much more robust reaction and volume of coverage. I didn't ask a lot of questions back then, didn't try to research or figure out what happened in any detail. I was just trying to deal with my own grief and help my mom as much as I could. In reflecting now, I wish I would have taken the time to find out everything I could have, perhaps that would have helped me work through my own grief in a much quicker fashion. It would have settled many of the lingering questions that I still have.

Willpower Is No Power

Willpower can produce short-term change, but it creates constant internal stress because you haven't dealt with the root cause.

—Rick Warren

I was in my early forties and in for my annual physical at the clinic. Sitting on the examining room table and talking to my family doctor, when I finally said "it." I told him . . . I thought I was suffering from depression. For some time, I'd been fighting it, trying to use willpower to overcome my feelings of sadness and self-doubt. I had finally come to the realization that I needed help. I was embarrassed to tell my family physician, but needed to tell him. I had to tell him and finally did. I had nowhere else to turn; I couldn't kick the feelings of sadness no matter how hard I tried. I felt very awkward and uncomfortable telling my physician. Imagine being a grown man telling another grown man about your innermost, deepest secret where you are totally vulnerable. It took a lot of courage for me to come forward. Thankfully, he was very understanding and gave me a referral to a counselor, Steve, to speak with.

I called Steve later that afternoon to set an appointment. He wasn't available, so I left him a message. I was parked on the side of the road a couple of streets over from my office when he called back a short while later. I briefly told him about my situation, that I felt as though I was suffering from depression and that I needed to talk to someone. I could barely get the words out as I was all choked up. Somehow the whole weight of fighting the feelings of sadness came pouring out of me emotionally at that time as I told Steve of my situation. We didn't speak for very long; he was understanding and supportive and we agreed to meet the following week. It was hard, very hard admitting to another man that I was suffering from depression. Heck, there I was sitting on the side of the road all tied up in emotional knots. Even though I had a wonderful wife, was the father of five beautiful children, had a very good job, was on the company board of directors, made decent money and had a nice home, it wasn't enough. I wasn't happy with myself. Unreal! I felt awful. I felt like I was an imposter, but I felt relieved as well. Now that the weight of the secret I had been carrying for years was off, I was hopeful that I could get some help to deal with it.

There were so many times when I didn't feel like smiling or being upbeat or acting professional or encouraging others. But I did my best to do those things because of my role as a father and husband and company leader. At this time in my life, I never thought or felt that I was accomplishing enough with the talent I had. I didn't feel as if I was living a significant enough life based on the goals I had set out to achieve. I compared my accomplishments and who I was impacting to my father's accomplishments and felt inadequate and inferior. He'd held so many leadership positions during his life; I held few. He had volunteered all sorts of his time to help others; I didn't volunteer much. I compared myself to other people who appeared to be successful and happy. It seemed as though everyone else was better off than I was. The continuous drain of feeling down at times but acting differently was exhausting. There was a constant battle going on inside me . . . fighting the way I felt on the inside with the way I needed to act on the outside. I was a living paradox for sure.

We've all heard the adage "where there's a will, there's a way," but in my case, that will, that willpower, just kept me stuck for quite a while. I felt as though I could push my way through and get over feeling down by myself, but it ultimately didn't work. Recently I've heard of the phrase "where there's will . . . there's a wall." I can certainly relate to that. I got caught up in pushing myself, literally forcing myself to feel good, but not ever really feeling very good, at least not for any long stretches of time. Ultimately faced with that "wall," I asked for help and finally got it. There wasn't any particular instance that led me to take this step, other than I had tried everything I felt I could by myself and had nowhere else to turn. Where there's "willingness," there's a way. I finally became willing to let myself be vulnerable so that I could receive the care I needed to get better.

Being a man, a husband, a father, and a company leader, I always thought I had to be strong, to be in control. Ultimately, life teaches us lessons, sometimes hard lessons to learn, but in trying to be strong it led to my extended suffering. I suffered in silence for most of the time, unfortunately. You see, men, or at least men like me, don't share much, don't open up much for fear of looking weak or vulnerable. What will people think? What's wrong with me? Will my kids, friends and family still respect me? I wanted to always appear confident, strong and in control. I thought that's what I needed to do and be and act. But those things, at that time in my life, were just a projection.

I was afraid to raise my hand and ask for help, thinking I could take care of myself by myself. But I'm not that smart or talented. None of us are, really. There are many other people who can help, those who are trained in helping us deal with whatever challenges we have. Whether it be something like depression as in my case or any other area of our lives, tackling a serious issue by oneself is, as I found out, not a great course to chart. The result for me was years of struggle. I suppose selfish pride had a lot to do with it. Image had a lot to do with it. Societal pressures had a lot to do with it; I thought about the dean's admonishment to "take it like a man," trying to be strong and keep my emotions to myself, to work it out myself. My own ultimate weakness, fear and belief about how a man should be and act had a lot to do with trying to deal with my situation on my own for so long, without seeking the help I desperately needed.

Counselor Visits

We're never so vulnerable than when we trust someone — but paradoxically, if we cannot trust, neither can we find love or joy.

—Walter Anderson

After the visit with my physician and his referral to Steve, I set an appointment for the following week. I felt a sense of hope and curiosity in looking forward to our meeting and wondered what the session would be like. I actually felt better right after setting the appointment, better because I had made a decision to do something different than what I was doing in trying to deal with my own feelings of depression.

I had never gone to a counselor or therapist before, so I wasn't sure what to expect. I was relieved to be going and one could probably say I was a bit anxious at the same time. Thinking back on it now, it's hard to remember each of the sessions I had with Steve or even how many months the appointments lasted. I would go to the waiting room and check in at the clinic, at the mental health area which I think was on the second or third floor. I never told anyone where I was going or what I was doing. My appointments were all during work and lasted about an hour.

The first time I went, I do remember sitting in the waiting area, praying I wouldn't recognize or be recognized by anyone I knew. I didn't want to have to tell anybody why I was there. I kept my visits a secret from everyone, except my wife, of course. That first time, while I waited for Steve to come out, I just looked around the waiting room, pretending to read a magazine and wondering what issues the other people had that were checking in or checking out. Steve finally appeared from around the corner. He was tall, had dark hair and wore glasses and a tie. We walked down the hallway, made small talk and then went into his office. His office included a desk, bookshelves and a seating area with a couple of other small tables. I do remember seeing a box of Kleenex tissue sitting on the table.

Steve and I mostly just talked. He asked me a few questions each time, and I tried my best to share with him where I was at emotionally and what I was thinking. It was hard to open up to a guy who I really didn't know at first, but I had to trust that he was a professional and that he could help me work through things. He was pretty laid back and easy going. I remember thinking to myself, "This is what he does all day? Sit back and just talk to people?" I wondered if he got tired of listening to people talk about their problems.

We talked about a lot of things, where I was at with and what I felt about my job, my relationships and friendships, where I saw myself and mostly about how I felt about my dad's death and the impact it had on me. I had to open up and share with him why I was feeling down and depressed. I hung my head a lot while I talked; it was hard for me to make eye contact with him. I felt embarrassed . . . here I was, a man in my forties, an emotional wreck on the inside, but having to constantly display outer strength for my family and at my job. I felt, in many cases, like an imposter. It was flipping exhausting. I was especially emotional when talking about Dad and his passing; it was a good thing that box of tissue was there.

I do remember telling Steve that one of my doubts about myself and something I thought often was "Would my dad be proud of me?" I didn't know his love as an adult and wondered what he would think of me and what I had become as a man and father. "Would he be proud of me?" I had to wrestle with that question. That question was very emotional for me. I was very insecure at this time in my life and I wasn't sure why. Not that the question really had any basis in logic, because for all outward appearances, I should have been able to answer that with confidence. I am a good father, husband, friend, and business professional. But I needed and wanted that assurance, my dad's assurance that he would be proud of me. Without him here, I wasn't able to hear his voice answering my question. Perhaps I'd been trying to live up to an image impossible to emulate.

There are only a few people who knew that I was depressed and suffered this condition while I was going through it at this time in my life. I only told my wife, two of my brothers and a couple of close friends of mine. I didn't want to burden my mom or my other siblings with my situation. I don't know in retrospect if that was the right approach or not, but it's what I did.

For each session with Steve, I would go to the clinic and check in at the mental health desk and then have to wait for him to come out and get me. Even though it may have only been a few minutes or so, it always was a bit of an anxious time. I was still worried about being recognized by other patients or health care professionals walking through the area. The time between checking in and eventually see-ing Steve always seemed long for this very reason. I wanted to keep my secret a secret. I felt relieved when he'd finally appear from around the corner and greet me. We always engaged in small talk as we walked down the hall into his office. Even in those brief encounters in the hallway I felt more at ease, at peace.

The sessions we had were emotional for me. I was really going outside my comfort zone in sharing my innermost thoughts about my life. That was diffi-cult. Yet, at the same time, when we finished talking,

I always felt better. I was slowly unloading some of the emotional and mental baggage I had carried for so long, for close to thirty years. I know that each time I left Steve's office, I felt happier and better about myself as I lightened the weight of that baggage. Talking and sharing my secret was therapeutic, albeit difficult at the time. I learned a lot about how I felt and thought and how I could become more self-aware of some things I could do to counter my thoughts and feelings. Just like there are professionals in every field and endeavor, there are professionals in the mental health area to help you and me work through things when life becomes overwhelming. I am grateful to have experienced Steve's counsel, his listening ear and his encouraging manner.

Twisted Thinking

Be kind, for everyone is fighting a hard battle.

—Socrates

The counseling sessions I went to definitely helped me. I always seemed to feel better after having time to talk things through and to reflect on my thoughts and what I was feeling. In hindsight, I wish I would have gone sooner and reached out for help earlier. One of the things my counselor Steve suggested to me was to pick up a copy of Dr. David Burns' book *The Feeling Good Handbook*. David Burns is a clinical psychiatrist who subscribes to drug-free treatments for overcoming depression, anxiety, and self-defeating attitudes. When I think of a "handbook," I think of something small, but Dr. Burns' handbook is a rather thick book, more like textbook size. Since Steve recommended it, I thought I'd take his advice.

I started reading it and doing some of the exercises in the book. I have since recommended this book to others who I thought might benefit from the mental exercises he uses, because they did help me.

In the book, one of the areas that particularly applied to me was a description of what he calls the top ten ways of twisted thinking that many suffer from while in a depressed state of mind. Some of my own thinking put me into a deeper mental hole. My own thinking plus dealing with thoughts of my father's life and his passing contributed to my mental state.

Many of the ten thought distortions affected me during this time and at other times during my adult life. Here are Dr. Burn's ten thought distortions as described in his book:

1. **All-Or-Nothing Thinking**—You see things in black-and-white categories. If your performance falls short of perfect, you see yourself as a total failure.

2. **Overgeneralization**—You see a single negative event as part of a never-ending pattern of defeat.

3. **Mental Filter**—You pick out a single negative defeat and dwell on it exclusively so that your vision of reality becomes darkened, like the drop of ink that colors the entire beaker of water.

4. **Disqualifying the positive**—You dismiss positive experiences by insisting they

"don't count" for some reason or other. In this way you can maintain a negative belief that is contradicted by your everyday experiences.

5. **Jumping to conclusions**—You make a negative interpretation even though there are no definite facts that convincingly support your conclusion.

    A. Mind reading. You arbitrarily conclude that someone is reacting negatively to you, and you don't bother to check this out.

    B. The fortune teller error. You anticipate that things will turn out badly, and you feel convinced that your prediction is an already-established fact.

6. **Magnification (Catastrophizing) or Minimization** – You exaggerate the importance of things (such as your goof-up or someone else's achievement), or you inappropriately shrink things until they appear tiny (your own desirable qualities or the other fellow's imperfections). This is also called the "binocular trick."

7. **Emotional Reasoning**—You assume that your negative emotions necessarily reflect the way things really are: "I feel it, therefore it must be true."

8. **Should Statements**—You try to motivate yourself with shoulds and shouldn'ts, as if you had to be whipped and punished before you could be expected to do anything. "Musts" and "oughts" are also offenders. The emotional consequence is guilt. When you direct "should" statements toward others, you feel anger, frustration, and resentment.

9. **Labeling and Mislabeling**—This is an extreme form of overgeneralization. Instead of describing your error, you attach a negative label to yourself: "I'm a loser." When someone else's behavior rubs you the wrong way, you attach a negative label to him: "He's a goddam louse." Mislabeling involves describing an event with language that is highly colored and emotionally loaded.

10. **Personalization**—You see yourself as the cause of some negative external event which in fact you were not primarily responsible for.

Once I started being more aware of my thoughts and recognizing what thought distortion they fell into, I was able to start working on my mindset. It wasn't easy, but the first step was just being aware of what I was thinking about and how my thoughts turned into feelings and those feelings ultimately drove my actions. For instance, there were many times when I had feelings of worthlessness and had thoughts of dying. I often felt as if I weren't doing enough, accomplishing enough or being all I could be. This fits into many of the thought distortions in the above list including labeling, minimization, should statements and emotional reasoning. At this time in my life, I didn't love myself enough to feel good about myself with whatever I was doing or whatever I was accomplishing or not accomplishing. I minimized my good qualities and focused on my weaknesses. That thought distortion led me further into a sad, depressed state and I didn't feel much like socializing when I felt this way.

To counter this negativity, the exercise I did was to become aware of the thought distortion (minimization). I would then write down all the negative thoughts I was having surrounding that thought. The next step was for me to examine the actual evidence of that thought distortion. I was able to write down many significant accomplishments and see them in print. That evidence counteracted my negative thought that I wasn't accomplishing enough. I had accomplished a lot, in fact.

Other times, and this happened when I was particularly down, I would roll over while I was in bed while trying to fall asleep and wish that God would take me home, that I wouldn't wake up in the morning because I felt so inferior and insecure about my life. This is another example of the thought distortion of minimization. I wondered how many people would show up at my funeral. I was very aware of my age at the time and how I was approaching my dad's age of 48 when he died and wondered if I would outlive that age . . . a sad waste of emotion and time in retrospect. Being aware of what I was thinking was a very critical part of the path of healing for me.

I can say that much of my thinking during the times I was depressed easily fell into one of the ten categories. Doing the exercises in Dr. Burns' handbook helped me on my way to healthier thinking. The negative thoughts didn't really go away but I was able to short circuit them and not dwell on them. I became much more aware of what I was thinking and was able to put those thoughts into one of the categories he mentions and see how distorted my thinking was. That led to better thinking and that better thinking led me to be more accepting of who I am. I became more at peace with myself. Being aware of my thinking helped me, and it can help you too, especially if you feel your thoughts fall into any of the ten ways of twisted thinking.

Sad Songs

For me, singing sad songs often has a way of healing a situation. It gets the hurt out in the open into the light, out of the darkness.

—Reba McEntire

During many times when I was feeling down and depressed, I would listen to a couple of songs that meant a lot to me. Some of the phrases in the songs touched me and made me remember my dad and the loss I felt. I can't say that listening to them really made me feel better, but more like it deepened the pain and thoughts of depression even more, which is an odd thing to do when I think about it. Why would I listen to songs that actually made me feel worse? It's strange, sort of like I was stuck in quicksand and couldn't get out. I needed to process the pain that I had internalized for so long, and I wasn't going to get out of that funk until I went through the pain, felt the pain, cried and was down for extended periods of time. I was at a time in my life where I knew these songs would add to my feeling of loss, but I wanted to listen to the melodies, the words and phrases because they had deep meaning for me. I was just so "in tune," so to speak, with the words in the songs. Perhaps I listened to these songs because I hadn't fully grieved. I cried when Dad died and I was sad, but since I was only 14 years old, I didn't really understand how to completely mourn his passing. In retrospect, listening to these songs was just one way in which I processed that grief.

One song I listened to was *Dance With My Father* by Luther Vandross, which was released in 2003. That song is about how, Luther, as a young boy, lost his father and the pain his mother felt. His prayer is that God would bring his dad back to life so that he and his mother could dance together for one last dance. The song has a great melody, I would encourage you to listen to it if you've never heard it. Some of the verses in the song that have special meaning for me include:

Before life removed all the innocence . . .
And I knew for sure I was loved . . .
Never dreamed that he would be gone from me . . .
Sometimes I'd listen outside her door and I'd
hear how mama would cry for him . . .
I'd pray for her even more than me . . .

When you're a teenager, you're probably aren't aware of a whole lot going on in the world and your surroundings; I wasn't. You pretty much think everything is fine; you really don't have a lot of perspective. When my dad died, everything changed for me and my family. I never considered the remote possibility that I'd lose one of my parents. Why would I? Up to that point, I don't think I'd ever been to a funeral of a close relative, let alone anyone else. I guess losing my dad was part of losing that innocence, which is why that line in the song has special meaning for me.

Knowing you are loved is a wonderful gift. I know Dad loved me and loved our family. He sacrificed a lot for us, worked hard and provided a good home and that's just one way he showed us his love. Having that assurance is a grace from God that can never be taken away. But, part of the pain is not having his love with us for all those years growing up, and even now. His absence is felt; it really is.

My grandfather lived next door to us. He was old, I thought, when I was little, but I never imagined that my dad would be gone from this earth at the age of 48, before my grandfather who died five months later at 91. Again, being a young boy, I didn't really have any perspective on life and death and age. Things just were; there wasn't a whole lot of deep thinking going on.

I can only imagine how my mom suffered. I know she grieved deeply, felt lonely and cried often. My mom and dad took a trip to Europe in March 1975 to celebrate their 25th wedding anniversary. The actual date of their anniversary was August 5th. We had a party at our house in August and our closest relatives, along with my parents' friends attended. We were able to take some pictures of Mom and Dad together and have those as a lasting remembrance. I know my mom was lonely after my dad died. As I previously mentioned, she wrote a lot after his passing in different notebooks. I think the writing helped her put her thoughts down on paper and was somehow therapeutic for her. I'm not sure; I never asked her about her writing, but I know it was important to her.

The only thing I could really do was pray. I prayed for my mom, prayed for our family, and pray for my dad that he is in heaven. I still pray for my mom. She has a difficult time putting complete sentences together because of her strokes. As I have already mentioned, Mom often asks about "that guy," my dad. I remind her about what happened, and she says she remembers, but I'm not really sure she does. So, I keep praying.

Another song that has impacted me is *Homesick* by Mercy Me. There are many lines in the song that speak to me. I could have included all the lyrics from the song because all of them speak to me at some level, however I decided to select just a few that have special significance.

If home's where my heart is then I'm out of place
Help me Lord, because I don't understand your ways
I've never been more homesick than now
In Christ, there are no goodbyes

*Lord, won't you give me strength to
make it through somehow*

These lines refer to me thinking about my dad; that's where my thoughts are and my heart is and until I'm truly home with him, I'll feel a bit out of place. It gets me thinking about heaven and eternity and the restlessness I feel sometimes.

Not understanding God's ways has a lot of meaning for me and probably for you as well if you think about many of the things that have transpired in your life. Why would God take away my father now? At this time? Why would I have to grow up without him? I certainly didn't understand and don't understand why to this day. But, I know that my ways are not His ways; my thoughts are not His thoughts. I hope and pray that the answers will be clear someday and I imagine that will be when I get to Heaven. I pray for that understanding.

When my thoughts turn to Dad, that is when the pain of loss and longing for him really sets in. I wonder what life would be like if he were still with us. That constant longing and thinking about him gives me that homesick feeling inside. There really isn't a day that goes by that I don't think about him, even though it's been over forty years since he's passed.

As a Catholic, the phrase about "no goodbyes" has special meaning too. I believe that God is always with us, you and me; He never says goodbye to us even if we turn our backs on Him. And so it is with my father. God hasn't said goodbye to him or me or my family. He's always there for us. He is eternal. I have faith in the Lord that I'll see my father again. I have to work to remember that and not to despair.

There is no doubt that the prayer within this song has helped me throughout my life when I have struggled dealing with my father's death. It is a prayer that I say often, or some form of it, because without God's help, I can't make it through the challenges this life has for me. There is a saying that if God brings you to it, He will bring you through it. I have trusted in that, even when it's been the most difficult of times.

Another song, with special meaning for me and my family is *Auld Lang Syne*. New Year's Eve was my mom and dad's first date, a blind date at that! This song is famous for being played on New Year's Eve at midnight, ushering in the New Year. It's a song of love and friendship of the past, and because it was special to my mom and dad, it's special to me. My dad used to always buy my mom a corsage for New Year's Eve as a remembrance of that first date. Each and every time this song is played it brings back memories of my mom and dad together.

Should auld acquaintance be forgot,
and never brought to mind?
Should auld acquaintance be forgot,
and auld lang syne?
For auld lang syne, my jo,
for auld lang syne,
we'll tak' a cup o' kindness yet,
for auld lang syne.

The meaning of "auld" is "old" and the meaning of "lang syne" is "long since." Take a cup of kindness refers to raising a glass in friendship and kind regard and in remembrance of noble deeds.

Another song that touched me during this time was *Heaven* by Los Lonely Boys. The guitarist in the band lost his young son to sudden infant death syndrome. The song is about the pain he felt in this world, waiting and wanting to see his son again. I think as you read the lyrics, the words are self-explanatory for someone who wasn't feeling very confident on the inside and was struggling with finding joy in the day to day. Here are some of the stanzas that affected my thinking and mood:

Save me from this prison
Lord, help me get away
Cause only you can save me now from this misery
I've been lost in my own place, and I'm gettin' weary
How far is heaven?

Certainly, there were times in the early 2000s that I felt I was in a sort of prison with my thoughts and feelings. I didn't like myself very much on the inside and felt like I was wandering through life at that point. I was in misery, with myself, my situation and was tired of the daily grind of putting on airs. I thought many times about wishing God would take me from this world. Many, many times. There were times I wished my struggle would be over, that the world would be better without me. How long must I go on?

And I know that I need to change my ways of livin'
How far is heaven?
Lord, can you tell me
I've been locked up way too long in this crazy world
How far is heaven?
And I just keep on prayin', Lord, and just keep on livin'
How far is heaven?
Yeah, Lord, can you tell me?

My thoughts weren't healthy, and I knew it. I continually struggled with them. I knew I needed to change. That's why this part of the song speaks to me. I needed to get help and eventually did, thank goodness!

When you are depressed, you feel locked up, stuck, feeling like you're all alone. It was a difficult time I was living in, for sure. I was trying to find myself, trying to move through each day with a purpose.

The last song is also by Mercy Me and was released in 2001. This song was written by Bart Millard, the lead singer and vocalist of the band, after his father passed away. He wrote the words "I can only imagine" on many different pages of his journal when thinking about his father. He imagines what it would be like standing before God in heaven.

I can only imagine what it will be like
When I walk, by Your side
I can only imagine what my eyes will see
When Your face is before me

I can only imagine
I can only imagine
Surrounded by Your glory
What will my heart feel?
Will I dance for you Jesus
Or in awe of You be still?
Will I stand in Your presence
Or to my knees will I fall?
Will I sing hallelujah
Will I be able to speak at all
I can only imagine
I can only imagine

Many times, I've wondered what heaven is like and what my father is experiencing in the next life. What a glorious feeling it must be for him . . . that is, if one can feel anything in heaven! With all my limitations, our limitations, we can only imagine what heaven is like for you and me. I can only imagine how the angels and saints welcomed my father into eternity. And while I am happy for that, I also long for it myself.

Secret Tears

*Sometimes in our lives, tears are
the lenses we need to see Jesus.*

—Pope Francis

When I was going through the hardest times, quite often I would reflect on Dad's passing while lying in bed, or in quiet times around the house. I would replay the words of his eulogy in my mind. I have memorized many of the parts since I've read it hundreds of times. It's then that I would get very emotional. My eyes would well up with tears. The emotions would come on me like a wave, a wave of sadness I couldn't suppress or prevent from hitting me. I'd go into the bathroom, close the door, and wipe the tears from my eyes so my wife and kids wouldn't see me upset. If you have gone through periods of depression yourself, I'm sure you can relate. If you haven't, then you may not understand. It's a power that I don't grasp or comprehend.

When those feelings come, it's as if I'm in mental quicksand. I am unsure of the reason the wave of sadness comes; it just comes. Perhaps I'm feeling sorry for myself, for the loss of not growing up having my father with me. Perhaps it's because I'm imagining the pain he went through during the explosion and fire. Perhaps it's because I might feel as though I haven't done enough with my life. Often, it's because I feel so sorry for my mom, who I know suffered greatly after losing her husband of 25 years, and then trying to hold the family together while we were growing up.

Not that any of this suffering is that unusual; it's more the way I dealt with it that I feel is somewhat unusual. If I'm in bed with my wife Peggy and the emotion overcomes me, I'll roll over to one side, to hide my eyes from her. I don't want her to see me cry or to see me upset. She doesn't know any of this, nor do my children. In fact, when they read this, I believe it will be the first time they'll even be aware of what has been happening in my life. I'm a master at hiding my emotions around my dad's death and the depression I've gone through. You see, men, maybe men like me, don't talk about death and certainly not about the death of a father. Maybe its pride or a lack of something within me, I don't know. We Joutrases didn't openly talk about how our dad died or the struggles we have had growing up and living without him. We just didn't for some reason and we haven't until recently started to converse back and forth via email about what happened and some of the memories we have of him. Maybe it's all just too painful to try to reopen those wounds.

I never considered getting help for depression early on because I thought I could overcome it myself. I think perhaps that societal mores probably had something to do with that mindset. Men in our society have this image of being strong, remaining strong for the family. Admitting my depression was a very humbling experience. Men who outwardly show their emotions, or admit their weaknesses are often looked down upon, or so I thought. Men often are the breadwinners, the leaders of a family; trying to keep up that image made my situation even worse. Worse because it took more time than it should have to seek help.

It's still hard for me even though it's been forty-plus years since he's passed on. My siblings and I still haven't had an open conversation about his passing and I'm hoping that maybe this book will be a step in that direction. At least it's a small step from me. And maybe for you too if you've lost a loved one and are still working through the grieving process and discussing the loss of your loved one with your family.

I have been able to share a little more about my dad and losing him with others outside my immediate family over the last few years. When someone would ask about Dad when I was much younger, I would mention he died when I was 14 years old, but not really talk too much about the incident or the challenges I had growing up. It's a bit easier now that I'm in my upper fifties. I don't stand out as being much different from others as I did when I was a teenager or when I was a much younger man. Lots of men my age have lost their fathers, so I have more in common with them; whereas before I avoided talking about it because I was unique in my situation.

Quite often I'll read my dad's obituary and the homily that Father Kaffer gave at his funeral Mass. Or I'll read the poem I wrote for my mom or I'll listen to a particularly sad song a couple of times in a row and that will remind me of my father and that will get me down. Maybe I do those things because it's my way of remembering him or grieving or just a symptom of me not ever coming completely to grips with his passing. You may think this is illogical, because doing those things would draw me deeper into a funk, but logic doesn't equate for someone dealing with depression. It's much more profound than just trying to apply simple logic. It's about coming face to face with who I was at the time, what I believed and how to deal with my sadness. You can't stop a wave in the ocean from crashing to the shore, and that's how it was for me with the sad thoughts; they came like a wave and I couldn't stop them. I just couldn't. Believe me, I tried.

I am sure that hiding my tears and feelings is based on pride. Trying to be outwardly strong during those times was hard, tiring and a constant struggle. Perhaps even a very selfish thing for me to do looking back at it now, because it kept me from enjoying more time with my family and friends. Quite often, I didn't want to do a lot of things socially. I'd go to work, maybe go to the gym and work out occasionally, but not a whole lot more. I can't change how I dealt with things in the past, but I can focus on moving forward in a positive fashion and dealing with my thoughts more constructively, and that's what I'm doing now. I'm not ashamed of crying and I'm not afraid to admit it either; it is who I was at the time. It is how I dealt with the grief.

Perhaps we'd all be better off if we let our emotions be our emotions and let them flow instead of suppressing them. Maybe we'd all be healthier or get through the pain faster. Sometimes I think I prolonged my own suffering by trying to be a strong man. I think that led to a more extended period of depression.

Regret

Regret is a form of punishment itself.
— Nouman Ali Khan

*I*n thinking back to the times and years I struggled with depression and sadness, I have learned some important things about myself and the situation I was in and want to share some of my lessons with you.

I made the mistake of focusing too much on the stem of thorns I was holding instead of my dad's rose. I was focused too much on myself, my loss and my pain. I should have focused on the bloom of heaven that Dad was and is experiencing. I can now admit I felt sorry for myself many, many times. I was filled with pride and suffered a lonely fate by not seeking help earlier because I couldn't get out of the private funk I was in for so long.

I think that trying to deal with issues as a man, without seeking help, is a fairly common thing. I regret the time lost not being happier. I regret not sharing myself more with my family and friends. Being alone was a way for me to try to deal with the grief and the depression I was in. In retrospect, it wasn't the best way to deal with my feelings, for sure. As the quote says, regret is a form of punishment itself.

Part of my purpose in writing this book is to try to help others avoid the same situation I put myself in for many years. Many times we might know what to do but we don't do it. We don't do it for various reasons: fear, pride, procrastination, lack of discipline or some other excuse. Asking for help is not shameful. It doesn't make you a weak person, regardless of what one might infer or believe by societal mores. It's one of the many lessons I've learned from all of this. Do not be afraid to ask for help when things don't seem right. Raising your hand doesn't make you weak; seeking help keeps you strong! And getting help will make you stronger.

So, if you've made it this far in the book, I would like to ask you a few questions:

- Are there situations in your life that you need to address?
- Are you afraid of what others might think of you if you shared your issue(s)?
- Are you feeling sorry for yourself?

If you answered yes to any of the above questions, it's time for you to take action, to talk with someone about how you are feeling, to become aware of how you are feeling and take a step towards getting better. Do it. Don't delay. Action helps to cure fear. Action changes things for you and me. The world needs the best version of you. Your family and friends and co-workers need you mentally healthy and happy so you can do the things on this earth you were divinely created to do.

I have thought about writing this book for quite a while, for several years in fact, but never thought I'd manifest that desire. I have tried to become more aware of the things I long for and believe that maybe God is speaking to me somehow through that longing. When I mentioned writing this book to several of my colleagues at a conference, they all encouraged me to write it and one even wondered out loud how many men I might help by writing my story. That gave me encouragement! So, I've taken the risk and taken the step to put my thoughts and a part of my life out there for all to see and hopefully to help you, the reader.

Regret would truly be unfortunate if one didn't learn from it and grow from the experience. Evaluated experience is the best teacher and that's what I'm trying to do here, to grow from what I've learned and to share with you. I'm done beating myself up over what could have been or should have been but am moving forward in a positive way. I don't suffer from periods of depression any longer. Do I have sad moments? Yes, but they don't linger and dominate my mind for days on end like before, and for that I am thankful.

Gravesite Visits

*He will wipe away every tear from
their eyes, and death shall be no
more, neither shall there be mourning,
nor crying, nor pain anymore, for the
former things have passed away.*

—Revelation 21:4

Visiting Dad's grave in Resurrection Cemetery in Romeoville, Illinois is always a difficult thing for me to do. When I stand in front of his grave and try to pray, all my emotions just come pouring out. It always hurts; it's always painful, it really is. But when I do go, I'm always glad that I went to visit, out of respect and love and maybe it even eases a little sense of guilt I may have for not going more often. I don't go as often as I should, and it's not as easy to visit more often since I don't live nearby the cemetery any longer. It's especially important to me that my kids have been along for several of the visits. I wish they could have known my dad, who he was, what he was like. I think he would have been a wonderful grandfather to them. That's also part of the pain, because they were not able to experience his love in their lives. It was really difficult when I first started visiting his grave, not that it's easy now, but I am in a better frame of mind to deal with the experience.

It's a surreal thing . . . going to a cemetery where your dad is buried. If you've ever been to a loved one's grave, you know what I mean. All the thoughts and emotions that have been suppressed come to the forefront while I'm in front of his gravestone. I usually break down, even though it's been more than forty years. It's still emotional for me. My dad's buried in the Our Lady section of Resurrection Cemetery, not too far from a group of shrubs and one of the roadways. It's probably not a coincidence that Dad is buried in this section of the cemetery. He prayed the rosary and I believe my dad had a special connection with the Virgin Mary. My dad painted the prayer "Hail Mary" while he was a young child and I have that artwork framed in my master bedroom; it's one of the special mementos I have from his life.

Years ago, my mom bought a bronze vase for my dad's headstone. The inscription on the outside of the vase is "Auld Lang Syne," a song whose title, roughly translated, means "for old times' sake." It's about preserving old friendships and looking back at the previous year's events. I mentioned this in a previous chapter about the importance of this song in Mom and Dad's life. New Year's Eve was a special time for them and they celebrated by going out for dinner and dancing each time the New Year rolled around. That's why my mom had the phrase inscribed on the vase. All the headstones are flush to the ground in the area where my dad is buried. The vase can be recessed into the ground when not in use, so the mowers can go over it without any trimming being needed. Even though visiting the cemetery is a spiritual and emotional place, I tend to notice these things out of habit, since I spent much of my career in the landscape industry. I notice these things and relate to how it impacts the time it would take the grounds crew to mow and trim around the headstones and obstacles.

The last few years, when I go to the cemetery, I lay a rose on his grave. It's in honor of Fr. Kaffer's analogy about death that he shared in my dad's eulogy. It's a reminder that I should focus on the bloom that death offers, that Dad is at peace, heavenly peace and that he's experiencing the fragrance of heaven.

The last time I went to the cemetery, I noticed an older gentleman standing there. His hands were folded in front of a gravestone in the next section to the north, praying. I felt bad for him, wondering if it was his wife that he'd lost. I wondered how long ago she might have passed away. I couldn't help but look over at him a couple of times. We were the only ones in the whole cemetery among acres and acres of headstones. I felt a connection with that man, perhaps because we were there for the same reason, to pay our respects and to pray.

This Side of Eternity

You must live in the present moment,
launch yourself on every wave, find
your eternity in each moment.

— Henry David Thoreau

As I've grown older, age 57 now, I've been spending more time reflecting on my own life, my dad's life and especially what the word eternity means and is. A thought about eternity is explained in my dad's eulogy. Fr. Kaffer tells the story about Bishop McNamara laying in a hospital bed and he said:

"We're all in eternity right now, and what particular difference does it make if we're in Rochester, or Joliet, or purgatory, or heaven?"

He goes on to say that once life starts, it never ends, an insight he gathered by watching the bishop go through a near death experience. Once life starts, it never ends . . . it goes on, it changes from this world to the next, and this is something that as a Christian is difficult for me to wrap my head around, but one I'm becoming more confident about as I study and grow and experience life. You and I are spirit first, gifted with an intellect, living in a physical body here on this earth. I do not fully understand the next life once my time on earth is done, but I do trust in it. I trust in eternity.

We all live on ***this side of eternity;*** this side is here on earth, the other side being heaven, God willing, or hell. I think most of the time we think of eternity as somewhere far off, the next life, but in reality, it's here and now. What we are doing and thinking and acting on in the present moment is all part of eternity. All we have is the present moment here on earth. Many times, I've been guilty of looking forward to the future, to reaching the next goal, to something else, rather than living more fully in the present moment. I'm not particularly good at living in the present moment but I am trying to get better at it every day.

We are living in eternity; we are part of eternity in this very moment. What my dad did and how he lived his life reflected his belief and faith as a Christian, a man and a father. I believe my dad's good works are echoing in an eternity called heaven; that's something I pray for and hope for myself, my family and my loved ones.

As Thoreau said, living in the present moment is a way of finding your eternity and fully experiencing it. I like that and am working on that. I hope you can too.

Ever Read an Obituary Like His?

A life well lived is a legacy,
of joy and pride and pleasure,
a living, lasting memory our
grateful hearts will treasure.

—Author Unknown

My family and the rest of the packed church sat in silence and continued to listen to Fr. Kaffer's homily. He had just finished explaining that life continues on after death and he shared his insights that once life starts, it never ends.

Father Kaffer then mentioned all the different organizations and associations Dad was involved with. He said:

"He also lived . . . here, with us. Did you ever read an obituary like his?

1. St. Bernard's School Board, Past President
2. Cantigny Post Bowling League, Secretary
3. Holy Trinity Council #4400 Knights of Columbus, Grand Knight
4. Providence Booster Club, Treasurer
5. Oil Chemical and Atomic Workers Union 7517, Secretary
6. Belmont Little League, Past Secretary
7. St. Vincent DePaul Society, Past Treasurer

"To say nothing of volunteer painter, construction worker, bingo helper, church lector, friend, neighbor, sports enthusiast, and husband, father, son and brother par excellence.

"To join so many organizations is a lot. To be active in so many organizations is incredible. To have leadership in so many organizations is faith-full, only a man full of faith would bother. So, not only do we know (by faith) he lives, this shows us how he lived. And it proves that he believed, because only a man full of faith, as I said, would bother. This kind of life, for others, would not make sense if God did not exist."

Growing up, I knew my dad was busy, but didn't really understand to what level. I was too young to grasp the level of his involvement in any organizations outside of his main job. I know at many times he worked two jobs. His main job was working at Union Oil Company in Romeoville, Illinois as an instrument repair technician. He attended classes where he received training for his technician role. He also worked a second job at times as a carpenter. As a teenager, I wasn't fully aware of all the things my mom or dad did in raising our family and the sacrifices they made.

My dad was also involved with the Holy Name Society at St. Bernard's parish and spent many an hour helping to build the new gymnasium and wrestling room at Providence High School, both of which were dedicated in 1977. He was also the chair of the capital campaign for building the new St. Bernard's Catholic Church in Joliet. All these things Dad did while raising seven children, adding on extra bedrooms to the house and taking us on camping vacations every year. He even raised rabbits, tended to his honeybees, made homemade ice cream and gardened so we'd have fresh fruit and vegetables to eat each summer and fall.

As I read the list of his involvement and the leadership positions he held, I can't help but think that God blessed him with certain talents, unique abilities, a willingness to get involved and help others and to do whatever he could, whenever and wherever he could. I believe God gave him these skill sets because they matched the mission He had for my father. I believe my dad used his talents incredibly well. God gives all of us a particular mix of talents and abilities that match up with the mission he has for each of us. I believe more than ever that when we long for certain things or we are discontented with the way things are, God is speaking to us in some way. I think we need to listen to our longings and discontentment, whatever that may be, to try to discern His message to us.

I admit that reading all the accomplishments and leadership positions my dad held is a bit intimidating to me. It's amazing to me that he held all those leadership positions and had a talent for fixing pretty much anything all while raising our family. On top of it all, it has made me think: Am I doing enough with my life? Or am I just settling? While he gave me an incredible example, it is hard to live up to what he did with such a short time on this earth. I know it's not fair to compare, but it's difficult to avoid. Am I doing enough? Am I accomplishing enough with my talents? Have I volunteered enough of my time and talent to help others? Is there a greater purpose for me that God has yet to reveal to me? These are some of the thoughts and questions that consume me at times, although I know I need to live my own life and not my father's or anyone else's.

I have even gone to the point of writing my own eulogy so that I can gain a better perspective and clarity around what I'm currently doing. I want to do all I can do with the rest of my time on earth. This has been a helpful exercise for me. It has helped me set some new, different goals and helped to identify some changes I need to make and am making in how I am living my life. It has helped me reflect on how I want to be remembered, what I want my legacy to be. I am trying to be more intentional about each day, the things I do, the impact I'd like to have. Writing out one's own eulogy is a stark reminder that we aren't going to be here forever.

My Dad's Rose

I like to think of death as a rose God gives to a family, but one He doesn't divide evenly.

—Father Roger Kaffer

After Fr. Kaffer read some of the activities my dad was involved in from his obituary, he continued:

"*We ask ourselves, again and again: Why? Why now? But why not now? Here is a man who has done more in 48 years than many do in 78. It's as though he's sitting on the bench and God, the coach, says: 'Lou, you've more than earned a berth on my squad. You've practiced hard enough; you've waited long enough. I'm sending you into the game . . . the unending life of heaven.' But that means that those of us left behind are going to miss his chatter on the bench.*"

The why behind the timing of my dad's death is a great mystery to me. It has been hard to understand why God would allow someone like my father to be where he was, when he was, on that fateful Wednesday. Like any of us, my dad certainly was not without fault. In hindsight, it sure seems to me that he gave to us and to others an incredible amount of service, value and love, and touched so many people in living his life.

There are a few verses in the Bible from St. James that I think are particularly relevant in this regard. St. James speaks of how one can show their faith through their deeds. He states that faith without deeds is dead; it's useless. He implores us to show our faith through our actions. It's not enough just to believe, not enough to just have faith. Even the devil has faith; he believes and trembles! But the devil certainly isn't saved. Father Kaffer's phrase regarding what my dad did, "only a man full of faith would bother," is really powerful and I believe matches up well with what St. James says in the Bible. My father didn't just go to church regularly; he shared his talents with those around him and he donated his time and talent and resources to help others. I believe his deeds were a great example of his faith in action.

Father Kaffer continued on:

> *"If you were here and Lou were there right now, would the priest be able to say the same nice things about you? If not, shape up. Your turn is coming and so is mine.*

"If you were here and Lou were there right now, would you and God be satisfied? If not, shape up. Your turn is coming and so is mine.

"As the poet said: 'Death comes with a crawl or he comes with a pounce. But whether he's slow or spry, it isn't the fact that you're dead that counts, but only how did you die?'

"None of these reflections takes away the hurt. Even Jesus wept at Lazarus' tomb. But if this unwanted encounter with death makes us think about how we're living and make any necessary changes, the good that Lou did for others in the past is even greater in the present: If this forces us to realize that the only sufficient reason for our life on earth is to get to heaven."

Those paragraphs about shaping up are a stark reminder to live in a manner consistent with our faith and beliefs. I want to do my best with the talents I have. I want to do all I can with those talents for as long as I live. I admit I often fall short of that ideal and that bothers me; it bothers me a lot. I often wondered when I was in my forties, if I died, who'd come to my funeral and what would people say about me and my life? I know that's a morbid thought, but there were times when I was down and feeling low that this was a common thought that would pop into my head. The church was packed at my dad's funeral and the procession of cars out to the cemetery seemed to go on for miles. He touched many people's lives.

One time I was watching the movie *Gladiator* and Russel Crowe, who plays the lead role as Maximus, is in the center of a Roman Coliseum-like building fighting other combatants to preserve his life. During a break in the fighting, he yells to the crowd, "What we do in life echoes in eternity." When I heard that phrase, it resonated with me and was another reminder because it made me think about what I was doing and how I was living. Our lives are short; my dad's life was very short, but what he did with his life mattered . . . it mattered then, and it matters in eternity, and so it is for you and me. And that's something for you and me to think about.

As Father Kaffer wound down his eulogy, I distinctly remember him saying these words:

> *"I like to think of death as a rose God gives to a family, but one He doesn't divide evenly."*

Fr. Kaffer was a gifted speaker and he leaned over the podium while giving his homily. I listened intently as he shared a powerful analogy about death. I can remember Fr. Kaffer speaking those words as if it was yesterday. I have read the last paragraph of my dad's eulogy hundreds of times. His parting words to us at my dad's funeral Mass impacts me even to this very day. I think his analogy of death being like a rose is one of the most beautiful phrases ever, and his final remembrance of my dad an incredible loving tribute to him. He continued:

> *"Your husband, Dad, son, brother . . . Lou . . . gets just the bloom of heaven, peace and joy. It's thornless; it's fragrant; it's beautiful.*
>
> *"You receive just the stem of thorns, painful thorns of loss; and they hurt like the dickens and they will.*
>
> *"But just remember: God could not give Lou his rose without asking you to hold your thorn.*
>
> *"God could not take him to Himself without taking him from us.*
>
> *"Concentrate on his rose as you bravely and lovingly and selflessly hold your thorn for him."*

God dividing a rose upon my father's death is an analogy that I have come to more fully understand over time. It's meaning is significant and while it's been difficult going through the grieving process, I appreciate Fr. Kaffer's words more today than ever. At the time of my father's death and up until my early forties, I was focused more on the stem of thorns, the thorns of loss. But those thoughts are very inward thoughts. I do not believe for a second that God giving my family a stem of thorns is any sort of punishment; it's just that His ways are not our ways. His thoughts are not our thoughts and we'll never fully understand God's ways or God's thoughts until we ourselves reach heaven.

"Just the bloom of heaven, peace and joy." I can only imagine what heaven is like and that Dad is living in God's presence and is eternally happy and at peace.

"It's thornless; it's fragrant; it's beautiful." Imagine heaven, if you can! What a glorious sight awaits us!

God could not give my dad his rose without asking us to hold our thorn. For sure, it hurts holding our stem of thorns. Painful thorns of loss -- that hurt like the dickens, for anyone who's lost a loved one, you know. However, I've now learned to be more focused on my dad's rose, focusing on the bloom rather than the stem of thorns.

Concentrate on his rose. Concentrate on your loved one's rose. It's beautiful; it's fragrant; it's peace and joy.

Way Forward

Remember forward movement. Forward is the way of trust. Forward is the way of forgiveness. Forward is the way of action. Forward is the way of healing. Forward is essentially life.

—Victoria Erickson

No matter what you are thinking about yourself or the situation you are in, if you struggle in any way, there is always hope; you and I must always remind ourselves of that. Even during the darkest of thoughts and darkest of times. There is always hope. I think part of my struggle may have been thinking things needed to be perfect and if it wasn't then I couldn't feel good about myself or the situation. I have come to realize that taking a step, no matter how small, is making progress. Even if you can't see the whole solution to your problem, take that step. Then another, then another. Soon you'll be on your way to thinking and feeling better. It took me awhile and it's a journey I'm still on, learning the way forward by moving forward.

So, what have I learned?

- I can't conquer my issues alone.
- Keeping everything inside hurts, really hurts.
- Depression is a real thing, with a lot of power to drag you down.
- There is help available.
- Most people are understanding if you just give them a chance.
- It's OK to talk about your problems.
- It's OK to cry.
- You don't have to be strong *all* the time.
- Most people won't think less of you if they know your inner struggles.
- Doing something–anything–about a painful situation is better than living with it.
- Recognizing you can't do it by yourself is OK.
- There is tremendous freedom in taking a small step forward.
- Serious depression is common. Over 16 million adult Americans suffer from depression each year according to the Mental Health Services Administration, and only one-third will seek help from a mental health profes-

sional, according to the National Center for Health Statistics.

- There is enough love even for me.
- It's OK to love myself more.
- There is a plan for me.
- I have value.
- I am worthy.

What would I advise as a way forward?

If you've made it this far in the book, then you've seen what I did, albeit late, to deal with my depressed state. I would encourage a few things to help one get unstuck. This is not a comprehensive list of recommendations by any means and obviously I'm not a doctor or trained professional, but I do think these will help, because they helped me.

Talk to someone about your situation. No one can help you if you don't share your situation. There are amazing professionals who are trained in mental health, just as there are doctors who help heal physical ailments.

Speak to your physician about your situation and what you are feeling and they can give you a recommendation or referral if needed.

Put your pride aside. Especially men. You can't shoulder everything, nor should you, alone.

Read about depression and its effects. There are many good articles online to help you better understand your situation.

Move around, exercise, don't remain stationary. Get outside, do something—anything—rather than sitting at home alone.

Do something social, even if you don't feel like it.

Get Dr. Burns' book, *The Feeling Good Handbook*, read it and do the exercises in it.

Read about the 10 types of twisted thinking. What evidence is there that what you're thinking is actually true? Replace negative thoughts with positive affirmations.

Meditate to help clear your mind. I didn't do this much, but when I did it seemed to help. Go on YouTube and find a meditation to follow along with.

Challenge your negative thinking. Become aware of your negative thoughts as soon as you have them. Ask yourself how those thoughts serve you. They don't.

Move forward; it's the way towards forgiveness. Towards forgiving yourself.

Final Reflections

> What lies behind us and what
> lies before us are tiny matters
> compared to what lies within us.

> —Ralph Waldo Emerson

When I first started writing this book, I didn't know how long it was going to be or how it was going to flow. How do I know when I'm done? I had set a goal to write this book, to tell my story, to try to help others. Then, I tried to set a timeframe around getting it done and the number of words I wanted to write. Those parameters didn't work too well for me. Setting a certain word number and date to be done was impractical. It didn't inspire me - it only stressed me out and frustrated me, and I felt some disappointment. It seemed like when I let go of those two goals, I was able to do better. My son gave me some good advice to try to write a little bit each day. I can't say I always did that, but it did help. I tried to write a little bit *almost* every day, even if it was only a paragraph or two. I wasn't on any deadline with a publisher so to speak, and only a few people actually knew what I was doing, so I didn't really have peer pressure, only the pressure I put on myself. But I have learned that writing a book is not an easy thing, especially for someone who's never written one before.

I admit having some fear over writing and publishing this book. What will people think? How do I go about getting it printed? What if no one buys it? And a lot of other questions. Ultimately, as I said in the introduction, if my writing has helped only one person, then my mission will have been met. Perhaps that one person is me. Or hopefully you or one of your loved ones. At a minimum, this book is a reminder of my dad's legacy, a way to honor him for the life he lived and the people he touched. I hope that by reading it, you have been helped in some small way. Perhaps it's given you some reminders of some great memories of a loved one you've lost.

As I think about what I've been through—the feelings of depression and sadness, the tears and the unhappy times—I have come to some additional conclusions that have helped me. Maybe they will help you also.

God has molded me through all I've experienced. And I'm still here being molded, trying to figure things out, trying to trust more and control less. The same goes for you; you are not a finished project.

I'm trying to be more present and enjoy each day because tomorrow isn't guaranteed, not to anyone.

Even though it was extremely hard at the time, ironically, those experiences have led to my growth. It has shaped me and I'm a better person for having dealt with sadness and depression. I experienced the pain and have grown from it. I have learned about mindset and faith and how to recognize and to dismiss negative thoughts before they take a foothold. I've become much more aware of my thinking. I have helped others when I recognize they are giving value to thoughts that don't serve them.

I've come to understand that I need to love myself first before I can more fully give of myself and serve others the way I want to. I've become much more aware of thoughts that serve me versus those that don't. I've come to understand and accept my shortcomings and faults; they are part of who I am, they just are. Yes, life is difficult. I've also come to understand I have some pretty cool things that God has gifted me, and I'm trying to be more thankful for those things.

Jesus has given us two great commandments: to love Him with all our heart, all our soul and all our mind, and to love our neighbor as ourselves. It's pretty hard to love your neighbor, to serve them if you don't love yourself. We (and me) have to be first before we can love and give to others. Be kind to yourself first. That's OK, it really is; it's not selfish.

Would God give me the gifts he's given me if he didn't want me to use them? Would He give any of us gifts He didn't want us to use? I don't think so. One of my gifts is my story, so I'm hopeful that in sharing it, it might help others.

God doesn't make junk. I'm not junk, and neither are you. I am worthy. He gave me the gift of life and special talents. Just the fact that both you and I are here is an incredible miracle. I had to stop thinking that I wasn't worthy. I had to stop comparing myself to others, even to my dad and what he accomplished. You are worthy, too, for the very same reasons. You have the gift of life and you have unique talents. There is no one like you or me and that's pretty special. Please remember that.

Concentrate on the rose in your life, the beauty and the bloom, the fragrance of living on this side of eternity. Make it a better place for others because you are here. I am trying to do just that.

Appendix

Eulogy

God didn't promise days without pain, laughter without sorrow, or sun without rain, but He did promise strength for the day, comfort for the tears, and light for the way. If God brings you to it, He will bring you through it.

—Unknown

The following is the complete eulogy Fr. Roger Kaffer gave at St. Bernard's for my father's funeral Mass. The copy of his homily is one of my family's most precious possessions. I have included it in the exact format Fr. Kaffer wrote it with the spacing and paragraphs as outlined, the only difference is his original version was in all caps… I imagine so it was easier for him to read from the pulpit.

Mass of the Resurrection
Louis Joutras—Oct 25, 1975
St. Bernard's Church, Joliet, Ill.

The only reason for our life on earth is to get to heaven.

Last Saturday morning at our varsity football Mass, that's what I told the team and coaches, before the Providence-Aurora game.

Last Saturday that game seemed awfully important (and it was, but only in a relative way). Lou, and many of you here today, watched that game.

There's another game today—against Walther Lutheran.

And many of you had planned to watch that game today, but you aren't. You're here instead, and rightly so. Because football games, and everything else we do on Earth, are only relatively important.

The only <u>really</u> important thing we have to do in our whole life, the only reason for our life on earth, is to get to heaven.

If you do that, your life is a success. If you don't, regardless of what else you may accomplish, you're a failure.

It is only in this context of faith that this week's events can have any meaning at all. As Cardinal Suhard said, A Christian is one who's life would not make sense, if God did not exist. Lou Joutras' life and death would not make sense if God did not exist.

This doesn't answer all our questions today, and don't wait with bated breath for me to answer them this morning, because I don't have all the answers, but I do have a few reflections I'd like to share with you.

The first thing is this, if you or I were God, we would not be here this morning because you or I would not have permitted Lou Joutras to be where he was, when he was, on Wednesday.

But then I think we must also admit that if you or I were God we would never have permitted the crucifixion, and once again we would not be here this morning.

But thank God, God is God—and we are not because there never could have been an Easter Sunday, with its chance for heaven for Lou and you and me, if there had not been a Good Friday.

As we prayed the first glorious mystery of the rosary, the resurrection while waiting for Joe's plane at the Joutras home on Wednesday night, we observed that we will never understand this week's Good Friday, until we reach our own Easter Sunday.

To put it another way—of all the living persons involved in this funeral Mass, only one can understand its mystery.

That one is Lou.

I'm not playing games with you.

I'm not trying to give you a snow job with words.

I'm telling you what Lou Joutras believed… and lived… and lives.

And I can prove each word: What he believed… and lived… and lives.

Let's take them backwards.

Lou lives. He no longer lives among us: He lives elsewhere, with God we confidently pray.

This truth of continuing life was most forcefully brought home to me by Bishop McNamara right after he had had a brush so close to what we call death that one doctor told me he saw him die three times clinically, as his blood pressure dropped to zero after open heart surgery.

I spent a few days with the bishop at one of the Mayo hospitals in Rochester Minnesota shortly after the operation. When I first walked into his room, he said: "It's all very strange." I agreed. He was weak, he was pale, and I presumed he might be delirious, so I let it drop and so did he.

Two days later we were alone in the room. By then I knew he was not delirious but perfectly sharp. The nurse was at dinner. Once again he said: "It's all very strange." This time I answered: "Bishop, you said that before. I don't have the foggiest idea what you mean." He explained: " We're all in eternity right now, and what particular difference does it make if we're in Rochester, or Joliet, or purgatory, or heaven."

From one who knew, not only from theology but from his own near-death experience, that the only reason for life on earth is to get to heaven. I got a real insight into life, once it starts, it never ends.

Jesus taught this, we believe him. Lou lives.

He also lived… here, with us. Did you ever read an obituary like his?

1. St. Bernard's school board (Past President)
2. Cantigny Post Bowling League (Secretary)
3. Holy Trinity Council 4400 (Grand Knight)
4. Providence Booster Club (Treasurer)
5. Oil chemical and Atomic Workers Union 7517 (Secretary)
6. Belmont Little League (Past Secretary)
7. St. Vincent De Paul Society (Past Treasurer)

To say nothing of volunteer painter, construction worker, bingo helper, church lector, friend, neighbor, sports enthusiast, and husband, father, son and brother par excellence.

As Father Poff observed yesterday, Lou wasn't just a joiner, he was a doer and yet always close to his family, extremely close.

To join so many organizations is a lot.

To be active in so many organizations is incredible.

To have leadership in so many organizations is faith-full, only a man full of faith would bother.

So, not only do we know (by faith) he lives, this shows us how he lived.

And it also proves that he believed, because only a man full of faith, as I said, would bother. This kind of a life, for others, would not make sense, if God did not exist.

We ask ourselves, again and again: Why? Why now? But why not now? Here is a man who has done more in 48 years than many do in 78. It's as though he's sitting on the bench and God, the coach says: "Lou, you've more than earned a berth on my squad. You've practiced hard enough; you've waited long enough. I'm sending you into the game... the unending life of heaven." But that means those of us left behind are going to miss his chatter on the bench.

I said to Dan, Bert and Dewey Ruettiger on Wednesday night that I think God sometimes suddenly calls to himself someone who is ready to come in order to shake up and to shape up some of the rest of us who <u>aren't</u>.

If you were here and Lou were there right now, would the priest be able to say the same nice things about you? If not, shape up. Your turn is coming, and so is mine.

If you were here and Lou were there right now, would you, and God, be satisfied? If not, shape up. Your turn is coming and so is mine.

As the poet said: Death comes with a crawl or he comes with a pounce. But whether He's slow or spry, it isn't the fact that you're dead that counts, but only how did you die?

None of these reflections takes away the hurt. Even Jesus wept at Lazarus' tomb. But if this unwanted encounter with death makes us think how we're living and make any necessary changes, the good that Lou did for others in the past is even greater in the present: If this forces us to realize that the only sufficient reason for our life on earth, is to get to heaven.

To Betty, Mark, Jeff, Ron, Mike, Joe, Steve, Chris and Pete… and also to Mrs. Joutras, Corinne (his younger sister, whom he loved to introduce as his oldest sister), Marilyn, Gerry and their husbands… On behalf of all of us, relatives and friends, I offer you our sympathy, our prayers, and I might almost say our holy envy… for the years of very close association you have had.

Now you, and we, must carry on.

Imitation is the finest form of praise.

You kids know, and I know that your Dad was at this communion rail every time he came to Mass. Never let a week of your lives go by without being here—worthily.

If you get down, and you will… get up, for you can. As you pray for him, also pray to him. We believe in the communion of saints. And here's a parting thought that might help.

I like to think of death as a rose God gives to a family, but one he doesn't divide evenly. Your husband, Dad, son, brother… Lou… gets just the bloom of heaven, peace and joy. It's thornless, it's fragrant, it's beautiful. You receive just the stem of thorns, painful thorns of loss, and they hurt like the dickens, and they will. But just remember: God could not give Lou his rose without asking you to hold your thorn.

117

God could not take him to himself without taking him from us. Concentrate on his rose, as you bravely and lovingly and selflessly hold your thorn for him.

Father Rog Kaffer
10/25/75

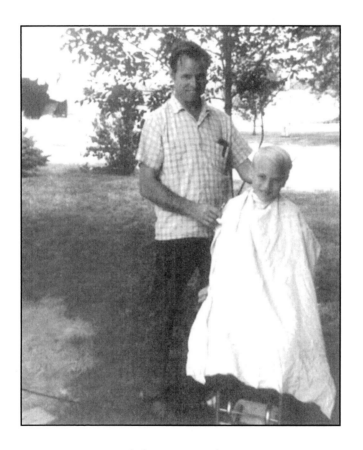

My dad giving me a haircut.
July 1971

My mom and dad with Grandma Joutras.
25th wedding anniversary Mass outside
St. Bernard's Church. August 1975.

My dad's army picture. He was stationed
in Germany after WWII. Circa 1947.

The Joutras kids. Oct 1964.
Mark, Jeff, Ron, Mike, Joe, Steve, Chris

Death is a challenge. It tells us not to waste time . . . It tells us to tell each other right now that we love each other.

—Leo Buscaglia

Every man's life ends the same way. It is only the details of how he lived and how he died that distinguish one man from another.

—Ernest Hemingway

About the Author

Jeffrey F. Joutras grew up in Joliet, Illinois, the sixth of seven children. Jeff now resides in Lodi, Wisconsin, where he enjoys spending time with his family, boating on the Wisconsin River and fishing for the elusive musky. He has been married to his wife Peggy for more than thirty years and is the father of five adult children - Clare, John, Benjamin, Aimee and Christopher. Jeff is a certified coach, teacher and speaker with The John Maxwell Team, and enjoys helping others learn about leadership, communication and personal growth. He loves public speaking and sharing his insights on life and leadership.

Why $13.99?

I priced this book at $13.99 because my dad used to participate in 13-run baseball pools with his coworkers. I thought it would be just one fun way of honoring him. I hope he's smiling in heaven because of this!

Joutras can be contacted at jeffreyjoutras@gmail.com